CULTURE IN ACTION

Roald Dahl

Jane Bingham

www.raintreepublishers.co.uk
Visit our website to find out
more information about
Raintree books.

To order:

☎ Phone 0845 6044371

🖹 Fax +44 (0) 1865 312263

💻 Email myorders@raintreepublishers.co.uk

Customers from outside the UK please telephone +44 1865 312262

Raintree is an imprint of Capstone Global Library Limited,
a company incorporated in England and Wales having its
registered office at 7 Pilgrim Street, London, EC4V 6LB
– Registered company number: 6695582

Text © Capstone Global Library Limited 2010
First published in hardback in 2010
Paperback edition first published in 2011

Edited by Louise Galpine, Rachel Howells, and Helen Cox
Designed by Kimberly Miracle and Betsy Wernert
Original illustrations © Capstone Global Library Ltd.
Illustrated by kja-artists.com
Picture research by Mica Brancic and Kay Altwegg
Production by Alison Parsons
Originated by Steve Walker, Capstone Global Library Ltd
Printed in China by Leo Paper Products Ltd

ISBN 978 1 406212 12 9 (hardback)
13 12 11 10 09
10 9 8 7 6 5 4 3 2 1

ISBN 978 1 406212 32 7 (paperback)
14 13 12 11 10
10 9 8 7 6 5 4 3 2 1

British Library Cataloguing in Publication Data
Bingham, Jane
Roald Dahl. – (Culture in action)
823.9'14
A full catalogue record for this book is available from the
British Library.

Acknowledgements

We would like to thank the following for permission to
reproduce photographs: A P Watt Ltd on behalf of Quentin
Blake p. **10**; Alamy pp. **12** (Graham Bell), **26** (Clive Thompson
People); Corbis pp. **19 top** (Skyscan), **19 bottom** (Tony
Savino); Getty Images pp. **6** (Popperfoto), **13** (Popperfoto),
27 (MJ Kim); iStockphoto p. **8** (© Markus Divis); Mary Evans
Picture Library p. **9 left**; Quentin Blake p. **18** (Reprinted by
permission of The Random House Group Ltd); Reprinted by
permission of The Random House Group Ltd pp. **5**, **9 right**;
Rex Features pp. **4** (ITV), **20, 21** (Jonathan Hordle); Roald
Dahl Museum pp. **7** (Dahl & Dahl), **15** (Dahl & Dahl), **22**
(Dahl & Dahl), **24** (Dahl & Dahl); The Kobal Collection pp. **5**
(Warner Bros./Peter Mountain), **14** (Tri Star), **16** (Warner
Bros./Peter Mountain), **23** (UA/EON/Danjaq).

Icon and banner images supplied by Shutterstock: © Alexander
Lukin, © ornitopter, © Colorlife, and © David S. Rose.
Cover photograph of Roald Dahl, reproduced with permission
of Rex Features (ITV).

We would like to thank Jackie Murphy and Nancy Harris for
their invaluable help in the preparation of this book.

Contents

Some words are printed in bold, **like this**. You can find out what they mean by looking in the glossary on page 30.

Who was Roald Dahl?

Roald Dahl is one of the world's most popular children's writers. He is famous for his amazing storybooks, such as *Charlie and the Chocolate Factory* and *Danny the Champion of the World*. He also wrote some very funny poems and two books about his early life.

Great ideas

Roald Dahl lived until he was 74. During his life, he had many adventures. He had some happy times, but some very sad things happened to him, too. Dahl also met some extremely strange people. These experiences gave him great ideas for his stories.

What's your favourite?

Altogether, there are over 20 Roald Dahl books for children. These are just a few of his best-known stories. Is your favourite in this list?

- *Charlie and the Chocolate Factory*
- *James and the Giant Peach*
- *Danny the Champion of the World*
- *The BFG*
- *Matilda*

Roald Dahl had a fantastic imagination. He wrote children's books for almost 30 years.

This is a scene from the 2005 film of *Charlie and the Chocolate Factory*.

Brilliant books

Roald Dahl's books take you on wild adventures. They have fantastic characters, like the Big Friendly Giant (BFG) and Willy Wonka, with his amazing chocolate factory. They also contain some surprising words, such as "Muggle-Wump" and "scrumdiddlyumptious". Roald Dahl's books can be scary, disgusting, and funny. They tell unforgettable stories.

ROALD
The Giraffe and the
Pelly and Me

Illustrated by Quentin Blake

DAHL

The Giraffe and the Pelly and Me is one of Roald Dahl's shortest stories, but it is still crammed with action and surprises.

Early childhood

Roald Dahl never forgot his childhood. Even when he was very old, he said that he could still remember exactly how it felt to be a child. Most of his books are told from a child's point of view. In *Danny the Champion of the World*, Danny tells the story of what happens to him and his father. In *George's Marvellous Medicine* you see all the adults from George's viewpoint.

Writing it down

When Roald was in his sixties he wrote a book for children called *Boy: Tales of Childhood*. It is full of stories about his life from before he left school.

A hero's name

Roald was named after the famous Norwegian explorer, Roald Amundsen. In 1911 Amundsen was the first person to reach the South Pole. No wonder Roald Dahl grew up dreaming of adventures! This photograph shows Amundsen beside the Norwegian flag that he planted at the South Pole.

This photograph shows Roald with his three sisters, Alfhilde, Else, and Asta.

A family from Norway

Roald's parents both came from Norway, but his family lived in Wales. At home the family all spoke Norwegian. Altogether, there were six children – one boy and three girls, plus an older half-sister and half-brother from his father's first marriage.

The Dahl family lived in a large, comfortable house, but Roald's childhood was not always happy. When he was three years old, one of his sisters died from **appendicitis**. Later that year, his father died. Roald became very close to his mother.

When he was young, Roald imagined that the Norwegian landscape was full of giants and witches.

Trips to Norway

After Roald's father died, the family went on holiday to Norway every summer. They spent part of their time staying with their grandparents. Then they sailed to an island, where they had a wonderful time, swimming, fishing, and sailing.

Witches and giants

Roald loved the wild Norwegian landscape. He also liked the scary stories of witches and giants that his grandmother told him. Later, he included giants and witches in some of his stories.

Norwegian fairy tales often include witches and magical animals. This is the witch Hennegraben and her magic hen.

A wonderful grandmother

In *The Witches*, the hero (who is never named) has a Norwegian grandmother. She is kind, funny, and brilliant at telling stories. This character was based on a mixture of Roald Dahl's mother and grandmother.

Cut it out!

A horrible thing happened to Roald while he was in Norway. He had very swollen adenoids (fleshy lumps between the back of the nose and the throat) so his mother took him to a doctor. The doctor cut out the adenoids with a knife!

Roald described this gory experience in vivid detail in *Boy*. He also put some gruesome scenes into his books. For example, at the end of *The Twits*, Mr and Mrs Twit get stuck doing headstands, until their heavy bodies squash into their heads.

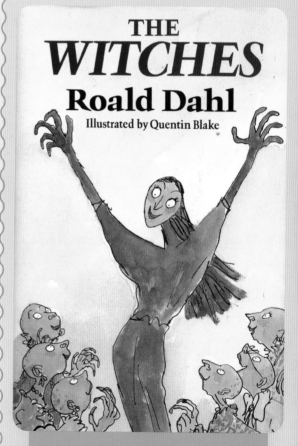

THE
WITCHES
Roald Dahl
Illustrated by Quentin Blake

The story of *The Witches* was probably influenced by the fairy tales that Roald's grandmother told him.

In this picture Sophie and the BFG are creeping up on the nasty giants.

The BFG

The BFG is one of Roald Dahl's most popular books. It tells the story of Sophie, who makes friends with a Big Friendly Giant (the BFG). Together they fight some very nasty giants, with names like Bonecruncher, Gizzardgulper, and Childchewer.

Different characters

As you read *The BFG*, you get to know the different characters. Sophie is sometimes scared, but she is always curious and determined. The BFG is gentle and kind. He has his own wonderful way of speaking, using words like "swizzfiggling" and "gobblefunking". The nasty giants are fierce, noisy, and violent.

Music for giants

Why not try creating music and dance for Sophie, the BFG, and the nasty giants?
You can work on your own, in pairs, or in a group.

Steps to follow:

1. What kind of tune expresses Sophie's character? How can you portray the BFG, and his strange way of talking? What sounds will you use for the nasty giants? You can clap rhythms and use your voices, or you can use musical instruments, such as a recorder and drums.

2. When you have made up your tunes, try creating dances for the different characters. You could make small, delicate movements for Sophie, and take huge strides for the BFG. The nasty giants could make heavy thumping steps, and jab their fists in the air. Use your imagination to think of other examples!

3. Read the chapter when Sophie and the BFG use the dream trumpet to frighten the nasty giants. Then try telling the story using your own music and dance.

Schooldays

When Roald was seven years old, he went to a school for boys. Every day when he walked to school with his friends, he passed a shop window filled with exciting sweets. It was the beginning of a lifelong passion for chocolate and sweets.

Beastly bootlaces

Roald loved liquorice bootlaces, but one of his friends told him a disgusting story. He said that the bootlaces were made from boiled and squashed rats. Roald didn't stop eating the bootlaces, but he did start thinking up ways to make surprising sweets.

This is Llandaff Cathedral in Cardiff, Wales, close to where Roald lived with his family. He went to Llandaff Cathedral School for two years.

When Roald was young, sweet shop windows were filled with jars of colourful sweets.

Trouble in the sweet shop

Roald and his friends spent all their pocket money in the sweet shop. He especially liked the massive gobstoppers that changed colour as you sucked them.

The only problem with the shop was the woman who owned it. Mrs Pratchett hated little boys. Can you think of some characters like her in Roald Dahl's books? (Try looking in *Matilda* or *The Witches*.)

A dirty trick

It wasn't long before the boys had their revenge on Mrs Pratchett. They decided to hide a dead mouse in the gobstopper jar to give her a terrible shock. Roald played practical jokes like this throughout his life. Many of his characters are fond of tricks, too.

Boarding school

At the age of nine, Roald was sent away to **boarding school**. He was very homesick, but he didn't dare complain. The headmaster beat his pupils with a cane and the school had a cruel **matron** (a woman who was meant to look after the boys).

Only one adult was kind to the boys. Mrs O'Connor read them exciting stories every Saturday. She also encouraged Roald to read a wide range of books.

Miss Honey and Miss Trunchbull

In the story of *Matilda*, there are two very different teachers: kind Miss Honey and horrible Miss Trunchbull. Some people think that Roald based these characters on the real adults at his boarding school. Miss Honey is like lovely Mrs O'Connor. Miss Trunchbull is like the frightening school matron.

This is Miss Trunchbull from the film of *Matilda*. Miss Trunchbull is mean and dislikes children.

Roald at Repton

Roald's last school was a famous boarding school called Repton. Once again, he had a mean headmaster who beat the boys, but Roald enjoyed some parts of school life. He was very good at sport and photography.

Roald and the chocolate factory

The best thing about Repton was the chocolate factory nearby. The factory owners asked the pupils at the school to try out their new chocolate bars. Roald remembered this delicious experience when he wrote *Charlie and the Chocolate Factory*.

When he was 13, Roald went to Repton School. He really enjoyed sport.

In this scene from the film of *Charlie and the Chocolate Factory* (2005), Willy Wonka is showing the children around his factory.

Charlie and the Chocolate Factory

Charlie and the Chocolate Factory tells the story of Charlie and four other children who each find a golden ticket that allows them to visit a chocolate factory. Willy Wonka takes them on a tour to see some tiny people, called the Oompa-Loompas, who are busy making sweets.

Surprising sweets

Willy Wonka's factory produces some truly extraordinary sweets. There are everlasting gobstoppers, marshmallow pillows, lickable wallpaper, and many more. Just imagine the fun of trying out Willy Wonka's inventions!

Sweet-tasting

In this **mime** activity, you can pretend to taste some of Willy Wonka's inventions. Then you can show the effects they have on you. Ask a friend to guess what kind of sweet you are eating, and to say what is happening to you.

As you start to eat, think about what **facial expressions** you will make. Will you smile, frown, or look very surprised? Then think of what you will do as the sweet takes effect. How will you move your arms and legs?

Steps to follow:

1. Pretend you are eating Willy Wonka's Chewing-Gum Meal, a three-course meal in a tiny strip of gum. First, you taste slurpy tomato soup. Then you taste chewy roast beef with crunchy roast potatoes. Last comes the sweet, gooey taste of blueberry pie.

2. Now try eating Hair Toffee. It comes in long, sticky strings, and as you begin to chew it, you feel an itchy tingling on your head and chin. Long hair starts to sprout!

3. Imagine you are slurping a Fizzy Lifting Drink. As it pops and crackles in your mouth, you feel lighter and lighter, until you start to float above the ground!

Adult adventures

After Roald left school he went to work for an oil company in Africa. He was very impressed by all the wild animals he saw. Later, he put many African animals into his stories and poems.

Flying high

Soon after World War II began, Roald joined the British Royal Air Force. He trained as a pilot. After one year of flying, he crashed his plane. He went blind for a few weeks and had to have his nose rebuilt. In spite of the danger, Roald loved the excitement of flying. There are great flying scenes in *James and the Giant Peach* and *Charlie and the Great Glass Elevator*.

The Enormous Crocodile is set in Africa and stars a crocodile, a monkey, an elephant, and a hippo.

Roald learned to fly in a plane like this.

Roald in the United States

After three years of flying, Roald was sent to the United States, where he worked for the British government. While he was living there, he began writing. During the next 18 years, he wrote many stories for adults. Like his children's books, the stories were often gruesome, with very exciting **plots** and lots of surprises.

Roald Dahl loved skyscrapers. *James and the Giant Peach* ends with the peach stuck on the spike of the Empire State Building in New York, USA!

19

This photograph shows Roald Dahl with his first wife, Patricia, and their children Olivia, Tessa, and Theo. (Tessa is the mother of Sophie Dahl, the model and author.)

Family life

While he was living in New York, Roald married an American actress, Patricia Neal. They were married for 30 years and had 5 children.

As his children grew older, Roald began to make up stories for them. In 1961 he published his first children's book, *James and the Giant Peach*. For the rest of his life, Roald concentrated on writing for children.

Moving to the country

Roald missed the British way of life, and around 1960 he decided to move back to England. The Dahl family lived in an old farmhouse in the village of Great Missenden, in southern England. Gipsy House had a beautiful garden and was surrounded by fields and woods.

Country stories

Roald loved the countryside, but he hated hunting and cruelty to animals. *The Magic Finger* and *Danny the Champion of the World* both tell stories of tricks played on hunters.

Sad times

The children of the Dahl family suffered some terrible tragedies. When Theo Dahl was four months old his pram was hit by a taxi and he was seriously injured. The next year, seven-year-old Olivia died from measles. Roald **dedicated** *The BFG* to her.

FLUSHBUNKINGLY GLORIUMPTIOUS

The Roald Dahl Museum and Story Centre is in the village of Great Missenden, where Roald lived for 30 years. It is a great place to find out more about Road Dahl and his books.

A lifetime of writing

Roald Dahl died at the age of 74. But he kept on writing until the end of his life. He had a special hut at the bottom of his garden, where he went to write and think on his own. He tried to spend four hours a day in his writing hut.

Short stories for children

Many people know Dahl's full-length books, but he also wrote several short stories for children. *Fantastic Mr Fox* describes how a clever fox tricks three stupid farmers. In *The Twits* some mischievous animals play practical jokes on the revolting Mr and Mrs Twit. *Esio Trot* tells the story of a tortoise and some magic spells. (Try saying Esio Trot backwards!)

This photograph shows Roald in his writing hut. He wrote his books sitting in a comfortable old chair.

This is a scene from the early James Bond film *You Only Live Twice*. Roald Dahl loved the excitement of the James Bond stories and in 1996 he joined the team working on this film.

Funny poems

Roald wrote three books of poetry. *Dirty Beasts* is a collection of poems about animals. *Revolting Rhymes* and *Rhyme Stew* both include some very strange versions of fairy tales. Just like Roald's stories, his poems can make you giggle and squirm!

Film scripts

Did you know that Roald Dahl wrote the **screenplay** for the James Bond film *You Only Live Twice*? He also wrote part of the script for the children's movie *Chitty Chitty Bang Bang*. (You can find out more about writing for films in the *Writing a Screenplay* book in this series.)

Words and pictures

All Roald Dahl's children's books have illustrations, and most of them are drawn by Quentin Blake. The two men worked very closely together. Quentin Blake was one of the very few people who were allowed inside Roald's writing hut.

Quentin Blake's style is easy to recognize. He draws in ink, using lots of scribbly lines to create a sense of movement and excitement. Sometimes he uses watercolour paint to add colour to his drawings.

Roald Dahl and Quentin Blake had a lot of fun working together.

Picture it yourself

Looking at pictures helps to bring a book to life, but you can also imagine the scenes in your head. Everyone has their own idea of how Roald Dahl's characters should look.

Steps to follow:

1. Listen to one of Roald's poems or stories being read aloud.

2. Now draw what you see in your head. It could be a character or a whole scene. Ask your friends to draw a picture, too.

3. Compare your picture with the ones your friends have drawn. Do the pictures look exactly the same?

Now try writing a poem or a short story of your own, and draw a picture to illustrate it.

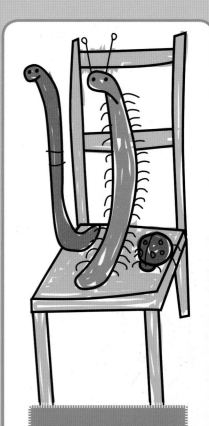

This picture illustrates a scene from *James and the Giant Peach*. Try to use your own ideas of how a scene should look.

This is an illustration for a made-up story.

A very special writer

Roald Dahl's stories reflect his love of adventure and his sense of mischief. When he was asked what made his books so special, he replied, "I only write about things that are exciting or funny. Children know I'm on their side."

Magic and surprises

Some people think that Roald's stories are like modern fairy tales. They describe battles between good and bad characters and they often involve some kind of magic. Some of them even have fairy-tale characters, such as giants, witches, and animals that talk.

The element of magic helps to create a very exciting story. It is also found in the story of *Alice in Wonderland* and in the adventures of Harry Potter. Are there other books that remind you of Roald Dahl's stories?

Roald Dahl's stories are easy to read – and they can make you laugh out loud.

Making jokes

In 2008 a prize was set up in memory of Roald. It is called the Roald Dahl Funny Prize and it is awarded to the funniest children's books of the year. It is a great way to remember a writer whose books are full of fun and jokes.

Fun with words

Roald loved having fun with words. Many of his characters have funny names, such as Augustus Gloop and Veruca Salt. He also uses fantastic made-up words, like "frobscottle" and "snozzcumbers". Why not try inventing some words of your own?

This is a scene from a play of *The Witches*. Roald's stories make very exciting plays.

Timeline

1916	Roald Dahl is born in Cardiff, South Wales.
1918	World War I ends.
1920	Astri Dahl dies from untreated **appendicitis**. Two months later Roald's father, Harald, dies from **pneumonia**.
1923	Roald leaves his nursery school, Elmtree House, to join Llandaff Cathedral School.
1925	Roald goes to St Peter's School in Weston-super-Mare.
1926	John Logie Baird invents television.
1927	Charles Lindbergh flies solo across the Atlantic Ocean.
1928	The first Mickey Mouse film is made.
1929	Roald goes to Repton School, in Derbyshire.
1931	The Empire State Building in New York is completed.
1934	Roald leaves Repton, and starts work in London for the Shell Oil Company.
1938	Shell sends Roald to work in Tanzania, East Africa.
1939	World War II begins. Roald joins the RAF, and starts training as a pilot.
1940	Roald crashes his plane.
1942	Roald is sent to Washington, USA, to work for the British government. He starts writing for adults.
1945	World War II ends.
1953	Roald marries Patricia Neal, an American film star.
1955	Olivia Dahl is born.
1957	Tessa Dahl is born.
1960	Theo Dahl is born. When he is four months old, his pram is hit by a taxi.
1961	*James and the Giant Peach* is published.
1962	Olivia Dahl dies from a serious case of measles.

1963	US President J. F. Kennedy is killed. A **vaccine** to protect against measles becomes available.
1964	Ophelia Dahl is born. *Charlie and the Chocolate Factory* is published.
1965	Lucy Dahl is born. While she is pregnant, Patricia has three strokes and Roald works very hard to help his wife recover.
1966	Roald writes the **screenplay** for the James Bond film *You Only Live Twice*.
1969	US astronauts walk on the moon.
1975	*Danny the Champion of the World* is published.
1981	*George's Marvellous Medicine* is published.
1982	*The BFG* is published.
1983	Roald and Patricia are divorced. Roald marries Felicity Crosland. *The Witches* is published.
1986	The space shuttle *Challenger* explodes.
1988	*Matilda* is published.
1989	The Berlin Wall is demolished.
1990	Roald dies, aged 74.

Glossary

appendicitis pain and very high fever caused by an infected appendix (a small, closed tube in the stomach). People can die of appendicitis if their appendix is not removed quickly.

boarding school school where pupils live. They sleep and eat there.

dedicated made or written for someone, as a special gift. Roald dedicated *The BFG* to his daughter, Olivia, who had died in 1962.

facial expression movement made by your face to show feelings and emotions. Smiling and frowning are both facial expressions.

matron woman who works at a school. Her job is to look after the pupils if they get ill.

mime act using movements and actions instead of words

plot story of a book, film, or play. Whatever he wrote, Roald's plots were always exciting and surprising.

pneumonia serious lung disease that makes breathing very difficult. Roald's father died from pneumonia.

screenplay written version of the words and actions in a film or TV play. A different word for a screenplay is a script.

vaccine something that is given in an injection in order to prevent people from getting a disease

Find out more

Books

All About: Roald Dahl, Vic Parker (Heinemann Library, 2003)

Here is a list of some of Roald Dahl's books, and when they were first published.
Charlie and the Chocolate Factory (1964)
Danny the Champion of the World (1975)
James and the Giant Peach (1961)
Matilda (1988)
The BFG (1982)
The Twits (1980)
The Witches (1983)

Websites

www.roalddahl.com
The official website of Roald Dahl contains lots of information about Dahl's life and books. It also has an interview with the author.

Places to visit

The Roald Dahl Museum and Story Centre

81–83 High Street
Great Missenden
Buckinghamshire
HP16 0AL
Tel: 01494 892192
www.roalddahlmuseum.org

The Roald Dahl Children's Gallery

Buckinghamshire County Museum
Church Street
Aylesbury
HP20 2QP
Tel: 01296 331441
www.buckscc.gov.uk/bcc/content/index.jsp?contentid=-1191581755

Index